7-DAY PRAYER AND DEVOTIONAL FOR THE GRIEVING HEART

Finding God's Peace in the Midst of Grief

VASTILLE EDMA

Copyright © 2020 Vastille Edma

All Rights reserved. No part of this book may be reproduced or transmitted in any form or by any means, electronic or mechanical, including photocopying, recording, or by an information storage and retrieval system – except by a reviewer who may quote brief passages in a review to be printed in a magazine or publication – without permission in writing from the author.

To my mother Marie,

Aunt Rose E.,

Aunt Rose D., and

my dear friend, Jason Randoo

who have all found eternal rest.

CONTENTS

Introduction 1

Day 1 3

Day 2 6

Day 3 9

Day 4 12

Day 5 15

Day 6 18

Day 7 21

About the Author 24

INTRODUCTION

Who am I to write about grief? The grief associated with the passing of a loved one?

I am neither a licensed therapist nor a counselor. However, I have experienced the death of my mother, my cousin and my aunt within the same year. It was a painful year for me and my family. It was hard for me to move forward, so hard that I almost lost my faith in God. During that period, I needed to be constantly reminded of God's love:

His loving arms were wrapping my frail
heart in times of distress.
God was wiping my tears of sorrow.

Was it easy for me to view God that way? Not all. It was a unique combination of consciousness and faith to choose God over my pain every second, minute, and hour. From that time, I understood how challenging it could be to pray while grieving the loss of a loved one.

This 7-day devotional is a prayer companion for those who are experiencing the loss of a loved one. It takes only a week or a quarter of a month to go through the devotions. It is also to remind you that you are not alone in your pain. You can find peace in God's love.

> *"He came and preached peace to you who were far away and peace to those who were near. For through him we both have access to the Father by one Spirit." Ephesians 2:17-18 (NIV)*

Your devotional time is purposely set aside with your Heavenly Father. Before starting each daily devotion, I encourage you to say the following prayer as an invitation to God's presence. This prayer is a gentle reminder not to take our time with God for granted:

> *"Lord, I thank you for guiding and allowing me to spend time with you at this moment. I welcome your presence during my devotion time. I pray that I will receive everything that you have for my healing, growth and love in You. Thank you for the light and the counsel of the Holy Spirit which guides me every day. In Jesus' name I pray."*

DAY 1

*When Jesus saw her weeping,
and the Jews who had come along with her also weeping,
He was deeply moved in spirit and troubled.
"Where have you laid him?" he asked.
"Come and see, Lord," they replied.
Jesus wept.*
John 11:33-35 (NIV)

When my mother went to be with the Lord, I felt that my pain was unique. As if, I was the only one in the world going through that terrible state of grief. Soon after, I joined a grief support group where I found myself weekly in a room full of other grieving women. Not only I realized that I wasn't alone in my pain, but also others were deeply hurting too.

If you are feeling alone in your pain, read out loud today's verses again about Jesus grieving the death of Lazarus. These verses in John 11 are reminders that Jesus understands your pain and your tears. Also mentioned was the community that came to share the pain of the family of Lazarus. These verses illustrate how Jesus and the community wept alongside the family.

During this devotion time, I encourage you to acknowledge that Jesus understands your pain. He can bring you a community that will grieve with you without judgement. It is always recomforting to talk to someone who can share your pain, at least someone who can lend a listening ear. Furthermore, believe that you can go freely to Jesus to get a hug, for in His arms you can wept freely. You don't have to feel alone; Jesus is moved by your tears.

Prayer

"Father, it is reassuring to know that I can come to you with full belief that you are not indifferent to my pain. You understand grief, for you had experienced it while you were among us on earth. Right now, I am hurting from the loss of [name of loved one]. It hurts not seeing their face or making more memories with them. Lord, I release my pain and tears to you. I thank you for the support that You are sending my way through friends, family members and even strangers. I welcome the healing and joy that only You can bring into my life. In Jesus' name I pray."

Moving Forward:

Listen to your favorite worship song.

DAY 2

*The Lord is close to the brokenhearted
and saves those who are crushed in spirit.*
Psalm 34:18 (NIV)

Today's verse is great to meditate on throughout the day, especially when the pain of grief hits. This verse confirms that God is ever present to comfort us, heal our broken heart, and strengthen us. Beyond everything we could imagine, it's reassuring to live with the certainty of a caring God. Moreover, He is willing to carry us when we are overwhelmed with fear, anxiety, or life's burdens. How can he save us? First, we should acknowledge that we need him. Next, we must believe that He will protect our hearts. Trusting God comes with faith. Let's exercise our faith during this time of grief to trust that God is near us, the brokenhearted.

Prayer

*"Father, I thank you that you are always close by
to save me from this overwhelming pain of grief. It's*

very hard for me to deal with the passing of [name of loved one]. At times, I feel like you are very far away, for it is so easy to be blinded by pain. Lord, I thank you for the sweet reminder in Psalm 34 that you are near me. Even when I don't think that I feel your presence, I will choose to believe that You are by my side. Amid this pain, You are giving me a testimony. I hand my day over to you, and may it be controlled by the Holy Spirit. In Jesus' name I pray."

Moving Forward:

Write today's verse on a piece of paper and read it throughout the day.

DAY 3

*Do not be anxious about anything, but in every situation,
by prayer and petition, with thanksgiving,
present your requests to God. And the peace of God,
which transcends all understanding,
will guard your hearts and your minds in Christ Jesus.*
Philippians 4:6-7 (NIV)

It is common to experience anxiety from the death of a loved one, whether it is anxiety about the future or the expenses for the funeral. During the grieving period, it can be easy also to fall into a state of loneliness or to forget our identity in God. Our hearts feel heavy. Our hope's battery level gets low. As we are going through this period in our life, let us remember the peace of Christ. As hard as it can be, let us remember to pray in a spirit of thanksgiving. It is so easy to wonder what is there to be grateful for. If there's nothing that you can find to be grateful for, at least be thankful for the peace that God promised in His words. Believe that His peace will overcome your anxieties and grant you solace.

Prayer

"Father, I am choosing to take you at Your word and to believe that You will bring me peace of heart and mind. I strongly desire to be with You, and I lift my prayer of thanksgiving to You. As I am mourning the loss of [name of loved one] and believing simultaneously in your peace, I pray that your peace will prevail over my mourning. Help me to remain positive and calm in the midst of adversity, for your peace is what I need on this journey. I declare boldly in faith for Your light to shine over the darkness of my anxieties. In Jesus' name I pray."

Moving Forward:

What current anxieties can you hand over to God?

DAY 4

When I said, "My foot is slipping,"
your unfailing love, Lord, supported me.
When anxiety was great within me,
your consolation brought me joy.
Psalm 94:18-19 (NIV)

Not only grieving the death of a loved one hurts emotionally, but also physically. I remembered when my mother suddenly went to be with the Lord, at times I would feel a sharp pain in my stomach. Grief is hard. Grief is exhausting. The toll that it takes on us sometimes leads to anxiety, or drives us to depression and sickness. However, knowing there's a God who will comfort us when we are anxious calms any fear.

As you are going through the days, move in faith with the certainty that God cares about your anxiety. He cares about your emotional or physical pain from grieving the loss of your loved one. Believe that God is ready to console you and bring you joy.

Prayer

"Father, I thank you for reminding me in Psalm 94 that you care about my anxiety; You won't let me fall into the darkness of anxiety. I find comfort knowing that you care about my situation. I also find comfort knowing that you are a good Father, to whom I cast all my cares (Psalm 55:22). Please hold my hands as I go through the days, most importantly hold my heart to stay closer to You. Be my guiding light this day and forever. In Jesus' name I pray."

Moving Forward:

How is God showing you that He cares?

DAY 5

Praise be to the God and Father of our Lord Jesus Christ, the Father of compassion and the God of all comfort, who comforts us in all our troubles, so that we can comfort those in any trouble with the comfort we ourselves receive from God. For just as we share abundantly in the sufferings of Christ, so also our comfort abounds through Christ.
2 Corinthians 1:3-5 (NIV)

The sudden death of my aunt, Rose, was very difficult for me to accept. At times, I didn't know how I would cope with the grief. As I started to believe that God was comforting me, I found the strength to volunteer with diverse non-profit groups and churches. When we are suffering, it is sometimes unimaginable to think of consoling others. Our calling in Christ is to be vessels of hope, love and peace. From the comfort that God is pouring into our heart, we should believe that we can pour into somebody else's life whether at work, a grocery store, or school. We must believe that we have something to give, for we are not alone on the journey.

God will purposely place people on our path to share from the peace that He has generously gifted us with.

Prayer

"Father, I am your vessel. In this time of grief, it is much easier for me to look inward and focus on my pain. Based on Your word in 2 Corinthians 1, I am choosing to believe that I have something to share with those who are suffering too. Lord, I pray that you will show me ways to share Your comfort with others. When those opportunities come up, give me the insights to seize them. I thank You in advance for every seized opportunity to show Your love. Beyond my pain, there you stand with peace and kindness, for You only are my provider. Thank you for this moment of prayer in Your presence. In Jesus' name I pray."

Moving Forward:

Name at least one person that you can comfort and how.

DAY 6

But the Advocate, the Holy Spirit, whom the Father will send in my name, will teach you all things and will remind you of everything I have said to you. Peace I leave with you; my peace I give you. I do not give to you as the world gives. Do not let your hearts be troubled and do not be afraid.
John 14:26-27 (NIV)

When the world mentions peace, it is usually associated with war, treaties or protests. In the new testament of the bible, on the other hand, peace is described as 'surpassing all understanding' (Philippians 4:7). It refers to a peace that the human mind cannot comprehend. Moreover, it is a peace that works in us through the Holy Spirit. In this sense, let us turn our eyes on Jesus who commands us not to be afraid in John 14:27. This is a command that can only be executed through faith, a strong belief that God can provide us His peace. Any fear that we may have of the future or the present has already been taken care of. Today, we choose boldly in faith not to allow our heart to be worried.

Prayer

"Lord, I thank you for the daily counsel of the Holy Spirit. In faith, I am choosing boldly not to be afraid. When sorrow, pain and distress fill my heart, I welcome your Holy Spirit to overpower those feelings. I will choose victory and peace, not because of my own strength but through yours. The loss of [name of loved one] is hard on me. Many times, I have felt depleted and abandoned. However, I know that my counselor, the Holy Spirit will remind me to place my hope and strength in You. When I don't remember Your promise, I will not feel guilty. I know that You will gently pull me into Your loving arms. In Jesus' name I pray"

Moving Forward:

List the areas of your life where you need the counsel of the Holy Spirit.

DAY 7

You turned my wailing into dancing;
you removed my sackcloth and clothed me with joy,
that my heart may sing your praises and not be silent.
Lord my God, I will praise you forever.
Psalm 30:11-12 (NIV)

For some of us experiencing the passing of a loved one, tears and grief are indisputably the same. A thought of the deceased or a ride by their favorite restaurant can bring tears to our eyes, at times uncontrollable tears. For others, those tears are internal. It may be that we take it on us to remain strong for the rest of the family or even our community. Does God care about our tears, whether internal or external? Rest assured that He cares.

How can we believe so? By taking his words in Psalm 30:11-12 that He notices our weeping and brings joy to our heart. During this journey, He will show us ways to honor the memory of our loved one without falling into deep sadness.

As the truth, the light and the way (John 14:6), He is guiding us from this season of pain to a place of faith in Him.

Prayer

"Father, I thank you for your words in Psalm 30. I thank you for your promise to turn my weeping into dancing. As I am experiencing this period of grief over [name of loved one]'s death, I know that you are guiding me and bringing me Your joy. I pray, Father, that you will show me ways to honor [name of loved one] on earth, not for my own glory but for your kingdom. I believe that Your joy is my strength (Nehemiah 8:10). I am fully confident that You will give me a dance along with a song of praise. Thank you for a fresh heart and a renewed joy. In Jesus' name I pray."

Moving Forward:

List three ways that you can honor your loved one, whether with your attitude or actions.

ABOUT THE AUTHOR

Vastille is a humble servant of Christ who desires to share her passion for prayer with the world. A globetrotter, she currently resides in Paris, France.

www.ingramcontent.com/pod-product-compliance
Lightning Source LLC
Chambersburg PA
CBHW010612100526
44585CB00038B/2642